A Look at Space

The Stars

by Rebecca Sabelko

BLASTOFF! BEGINNERS,
AN IMPRINT OF
BELLWETHER MEDIA
BY FLUTTERBEE

Blastoff! Beginners are developed by literacy experts and educators to meet the needs of early readers. These engaging informational texts support young children as they begin reading about their world. Through simple language and high frequency words paired with crisp, colorful photos, Blastoff! Beginners launch young readers into the universe of independent reading.

Sight Words in This Book

a	blue	long	red	up
and	can	made	than	white
are	have	make	the	yellow
as	in	more	they	
be	is	of	time	

This edition first published in 2027 by Bellwether Media, Inc.

Bellwether Media is a division of FlutterBee Education Group.

For information regarding permission, write to Bellwether Media, Inc., Attention: Permissions Department, 3500 American Blvd W, Suite 150, Bloomington, MN 55431.

Library of Congress Cataloging-in-Publication Data

Names: Sabelko, Rebecca author
Title: The stars / by Rebecca Sabelko.
Description: Minneapolis, Minnesota : Bellwether Media, Inc, 2027. | Series: A look at space | Includes bibliographical references and index. | Audience: Ages 4-7 | Audience: Grades K-1 | Summary: "Developed by literacy experts and educators for students in PreK through grade two, this book introduces beginning readers to the stars through simple, predictable text and related photos"-- Provided by publisher.
Identifiers: LCCN 2026011459 (print) | LCCN 2026011460 (ebook) | ISBN 9798893049930 library binding | ISBN 9798898802783 (paperback) | ISBN 9798898801359 (ebook) Subjects: LCSH: Stars
Classification: LCC QB801.7 .S225 2026 (print) | LCC QB801.7 (ebook)
LC record available at https://lccn.loc.gov/2026011459
LC ebook record available at https://lccn.loc.gov/2026011460

ISBN: 9798893049930 (hardcover)
ISBN: 9798898802783 (paperback)
ISBN: 9798898801359 (ebook)

Editor: Suzane Nguyen Designer: Laura Sowers

Printed in the United States of America, North Mankato, MN.

Table of Contents

The night sky
is dark.
Stars light up
the night!

The Stars

Stars are round. They are made of **gas**.

Stars are found in **galaxies**.

galaxies

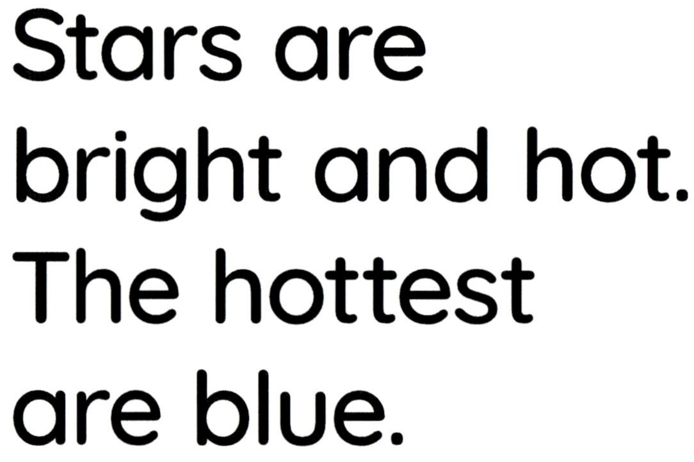

Stars are
bright and hot.
The hottest
are blue.

Stars can also be white, yellow, orange, or red.

Life of a Star

Galaxies can have more than 100 billion stars.

Stars begin as clouds of gas and **dust**.

cloud

Gases press together.
They make heat.
Stars shine!

Stars shine
for a long time.
They shine bright!

About the Stars

Colors of the Stars

What Stars Do

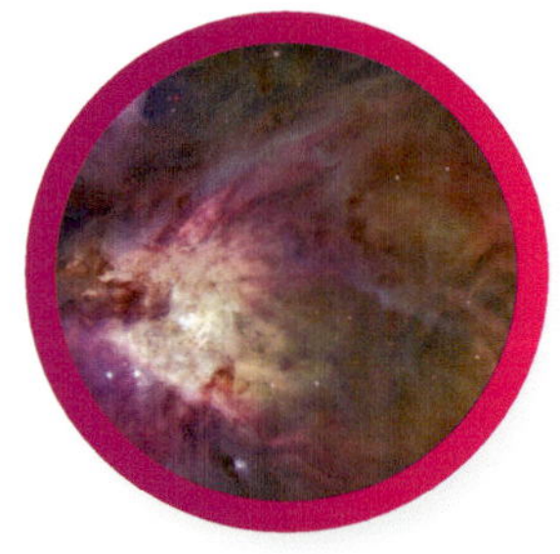

begin as gas and dust

make heat

shine bright

Glossary

tiny, dry pieces of rock

groupings of gas, dust, planets, and stars

something that does not keep its size or shape

To Learn More

ON THE WEB

FACTSURFER

Factsurfer.com gives you a safe, fun way to find more information.

1. Go to www.factsurfer.com.
2. Enter "the stars" into the search box and click 🔍.
3. Select your book cover to see a list of related content.

Index

The images in this book are reproduced through the courtesy of: shufilm, front cover, p. 3; Wirestock Creators, pp. 4-5; ESA/ Hubble & NASA, O. De Marco; Acknowledgment: M.H. Özsaraç/ Flickr, pp. 6-7; NASA and the Hubble Heritage Team (STScI)/ Flickr, pp. 8-9; Roberto Mura/ Wikipedia, pp. 10-11; NASA, ESA, and Don Figer (STScI)/ Flickr, pp. 12-13; Scott Book, pp. 14-15; NASA/ ESA and Hui Yang (University of Illinois)/ Flickr, pp. 16-17; NASA, ESA, the Hubble Heritage Team (STScI/AURA), A. Nota (ESA/STScI), and the Westerlund 2 Science Team/ Flickr, pp. 18-19; Xalanx, pp. 20-21; NASA, ESA, Massimo Robberto (STScI, ESA), Hubble Space Telescope Orion Treasury Project Team, p. 22 (begin as gas and dust); Wolfgang Brandner (JPL/IPAC), Eva K. Grebel (Univ. Washington), You-Hua Chu (Univ. Illinois Urbana-Champaign), and NASA/ Flickr, p. 22 (make heat); NASA/ Jeffrey Newman (UC Berkeley)/ Flickr, p. 22 (shine bright); Ekaterina, p. 23 (dust); NASA Goddard Space Flight Center from Greenbelt, MD, USA/ Wikipedia, p. 23 (galaxies); NASA, ESA, STScI, J. Hester and P. Scowen (Arizona State University), p. 23 (gas).